60 PROGRESSIVE SOLOS FOR
Classical Guitar

W9-CDJ-485

FEATURING THE MUSIC OF THE WORLD'S GREATEST COMPOSERS:

Bach, Handel, Mozart, Beethoven, and Brahms

Arranged by Mark Phillips

ISBN 1-57560-628-3

Visit our website at www.cherrylane.com

CONTENTS

These pieces are organized in order of difficulty within each composer's section.

Air

Johann Sebastian Bach

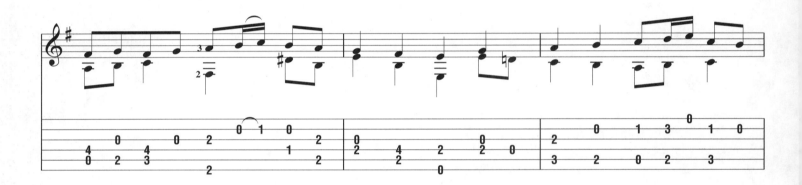

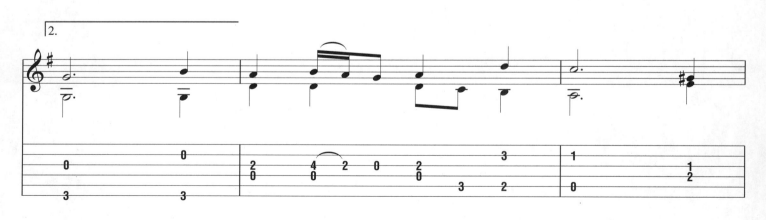

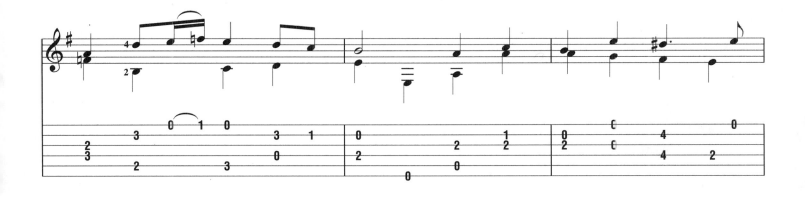

Bourrée

Johann Sebastian Bach

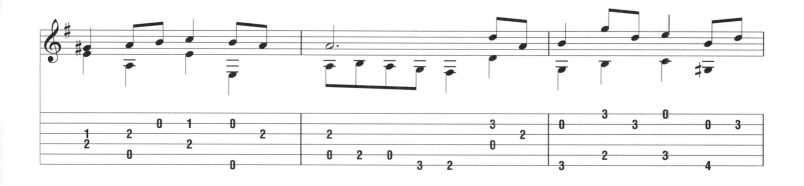

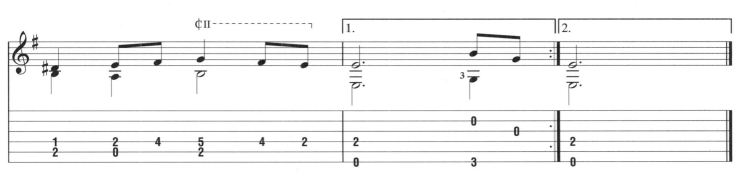

March

from the Notebook for Anna Magdelena

Johann Sebastian Bach

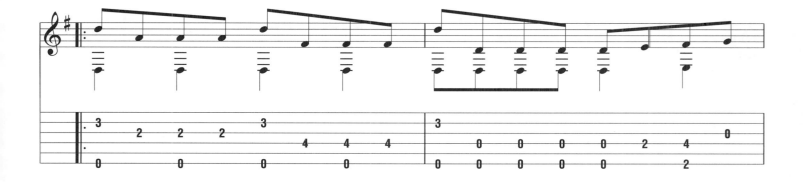

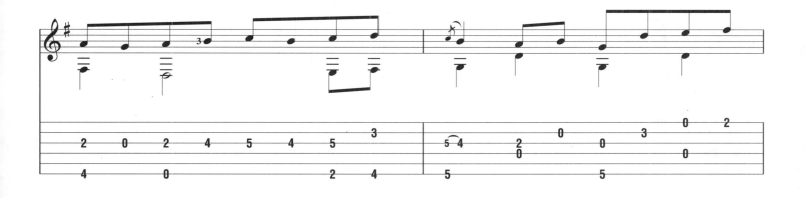

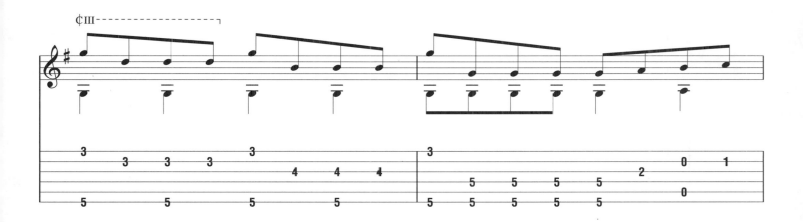

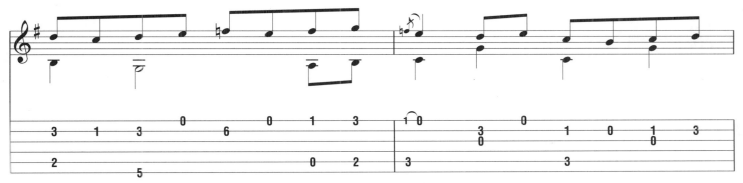

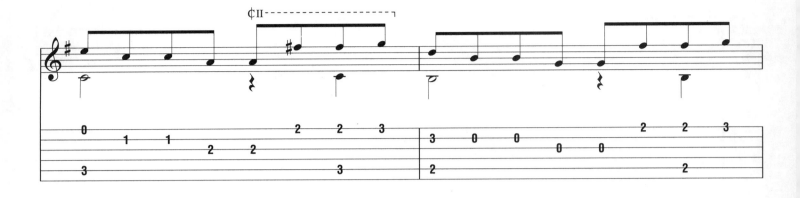

Minuet 1

Johann Sebastian Bach

TRACK 4

Minuet 2

Johann Sebastian Bach

TRACK 5

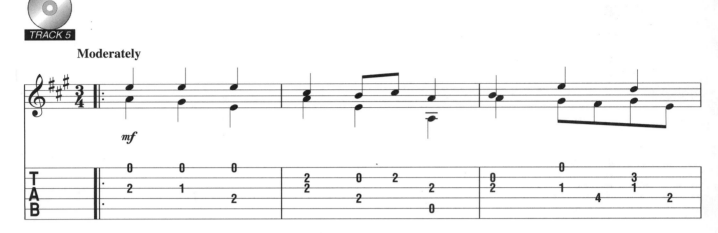

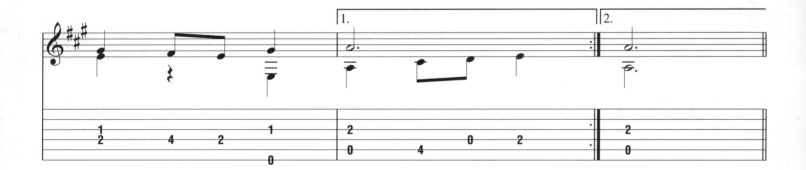

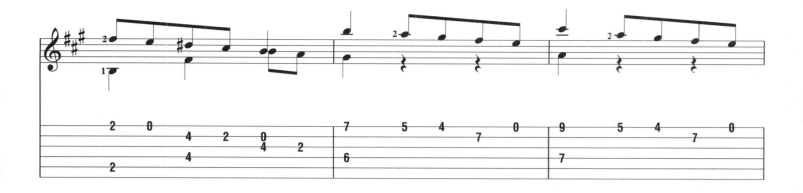

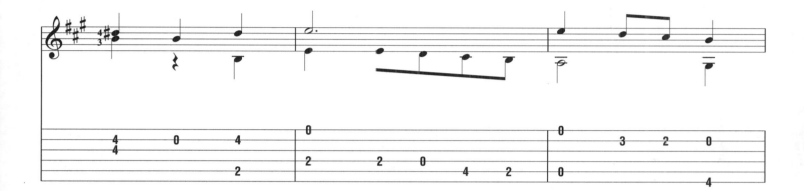

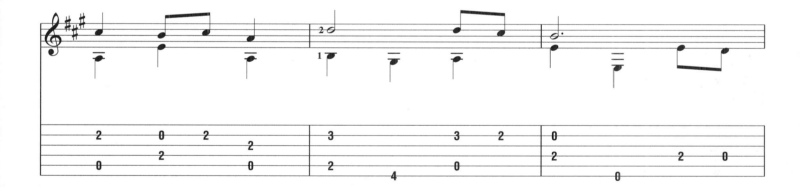

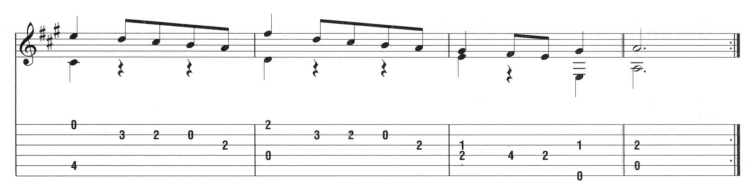

Minuet 3

from the Notebook for Anna Magdelena

Johann Sebastian Bach

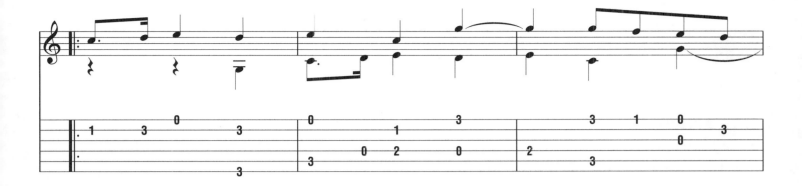

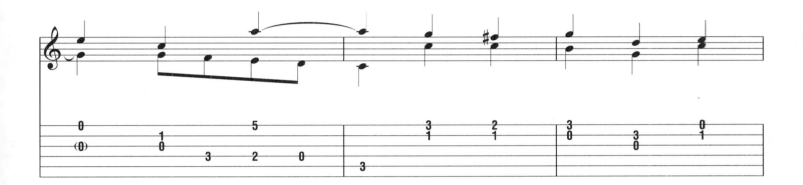

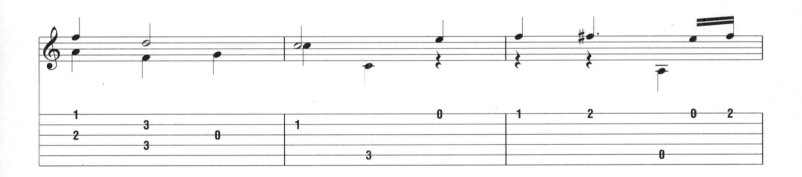

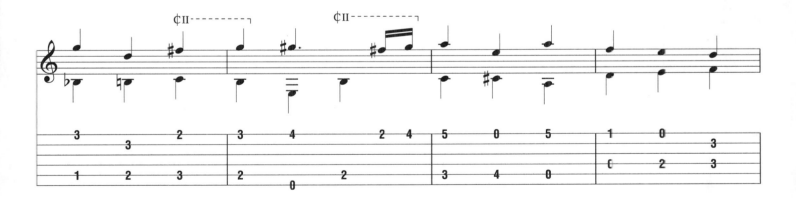

Minuet 4

Johann Sebastian Bach

TRACK 7

Moderately

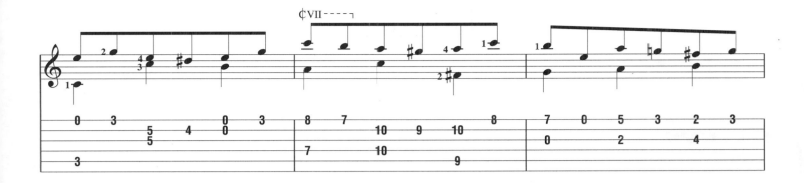

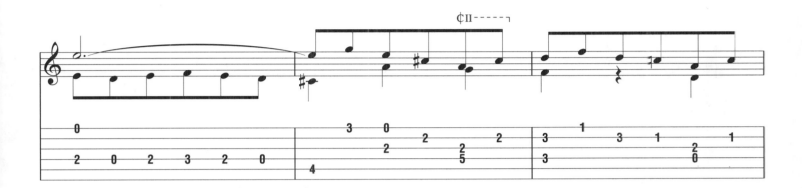

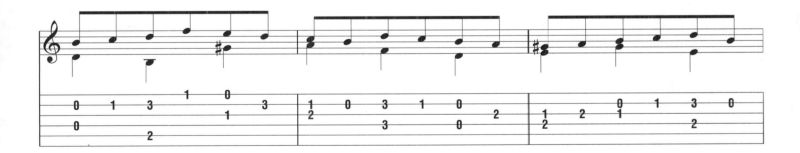

Minuet 5

from the Notebook for Anna Magdelena

Johann Sebastian Bach

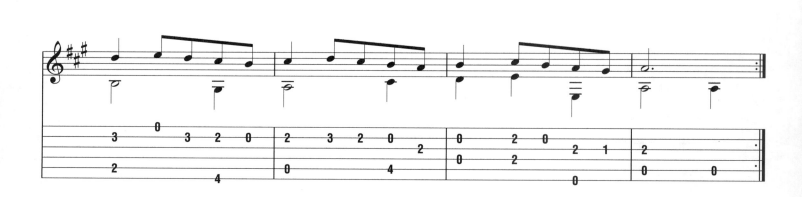

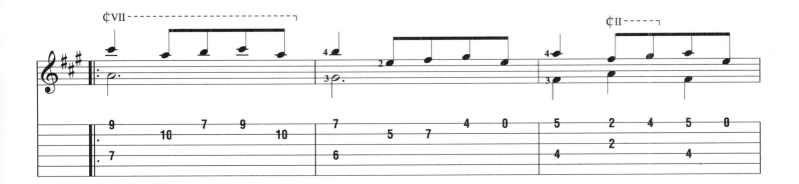

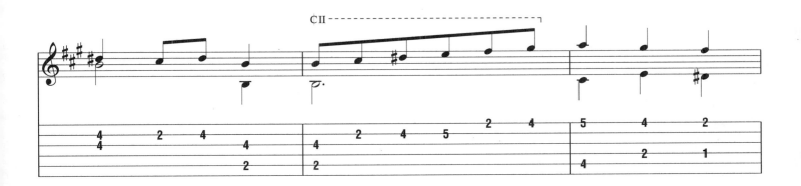

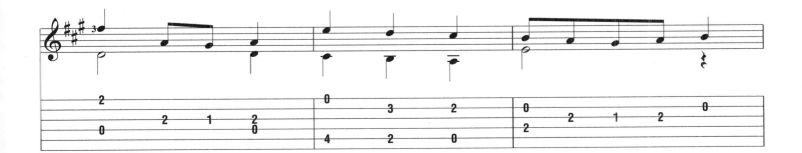

Minuet 6

from the Notebook for Anna Magdelena

Johann Sebastian Bach

TRACK 9

Tune 6th string to D

Moderately

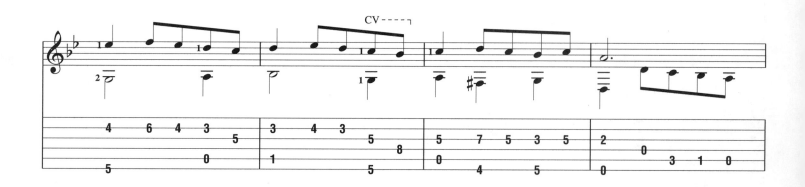

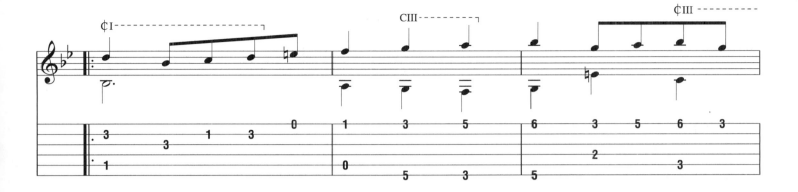

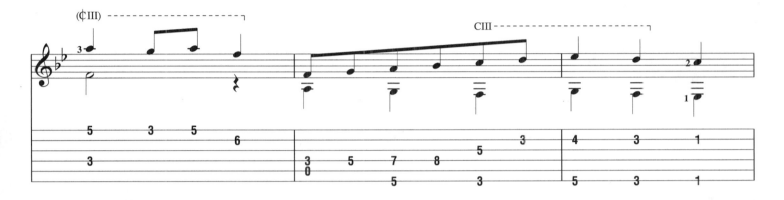

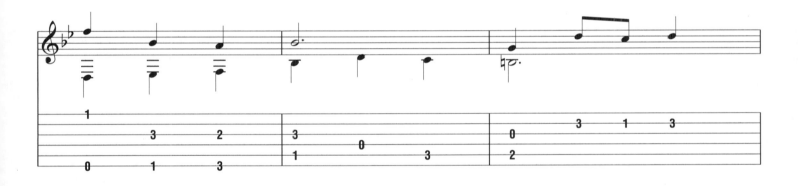

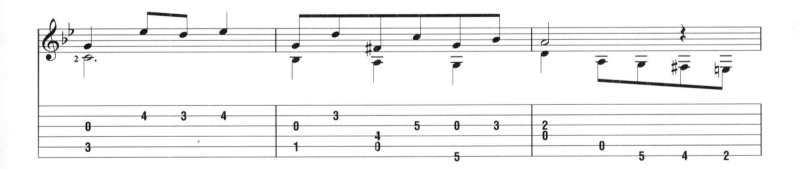

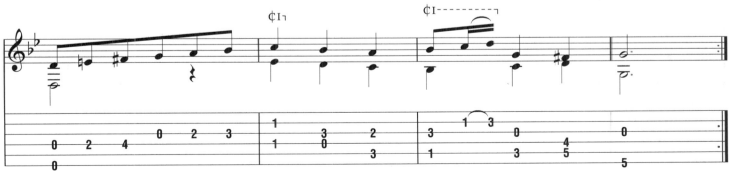

Air
(Originally Untitled)
from the Notebook for Anna Magdelena

Johann Sebastian Bach

TRACK 10

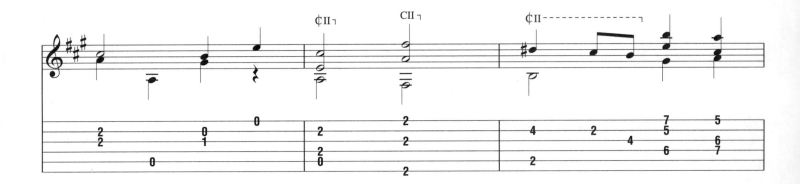

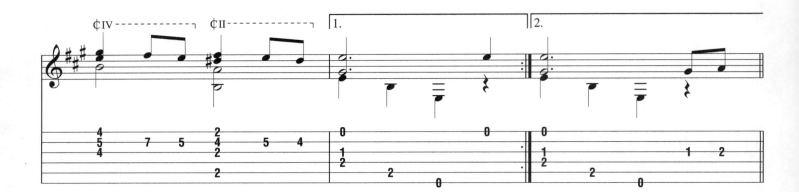

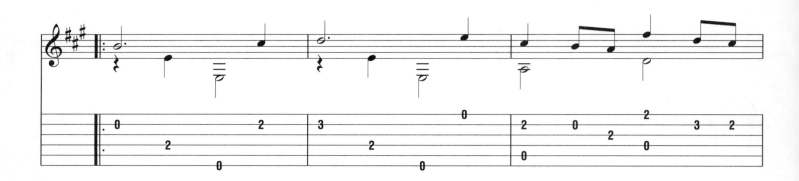

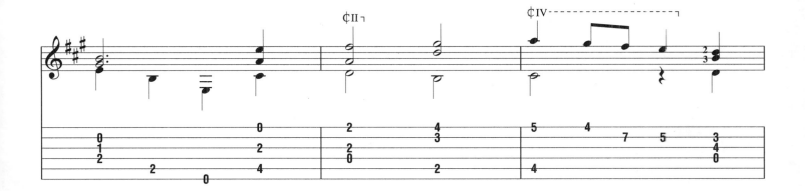

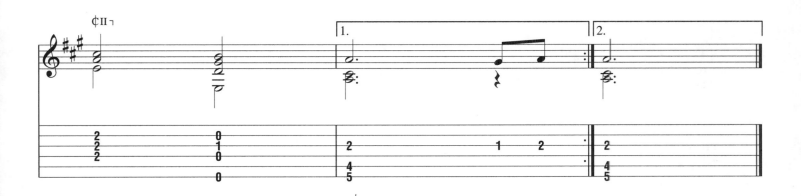

A Child Is Born in Bethlehem

from Cantata No. 65

Johann Sebastian Bach

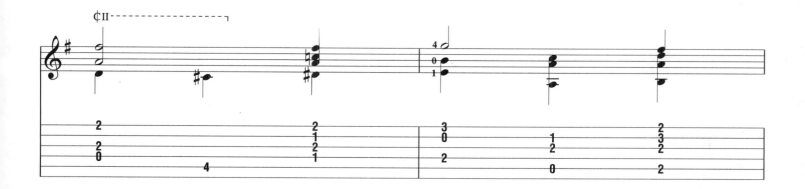

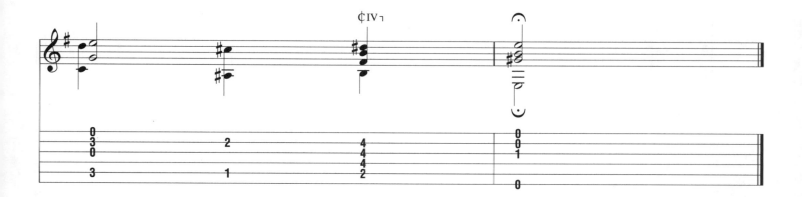

Chorale

from the Notebook for Anna Magdelena

Johann Sebastian Bach

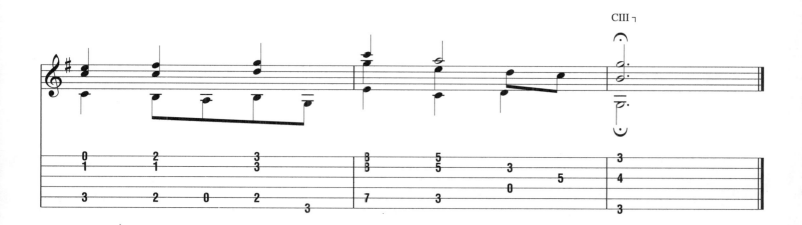

Jesu, Joy of Man's Desiring

Johann Sebastian Bach

TRACK 13

Tune 6th string to D

Moderately slow

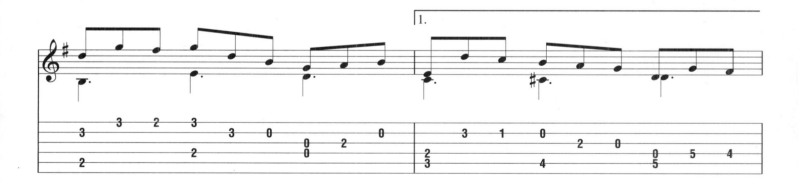

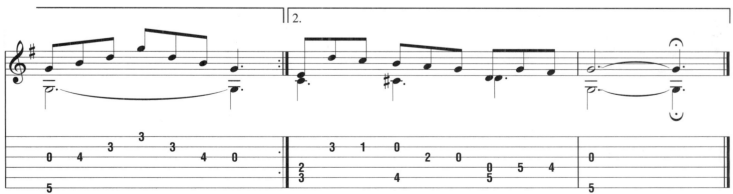

Jesu, Meine Freude
(Chorale)

Johann Sebastian Bach

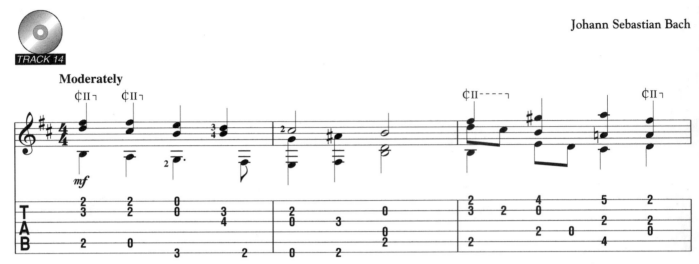

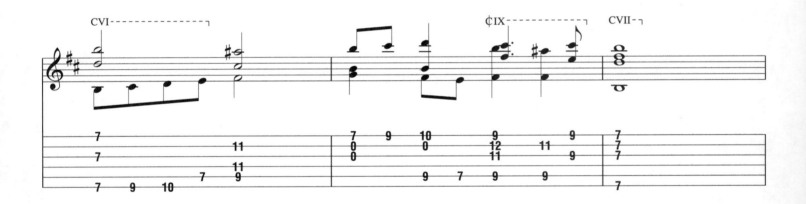

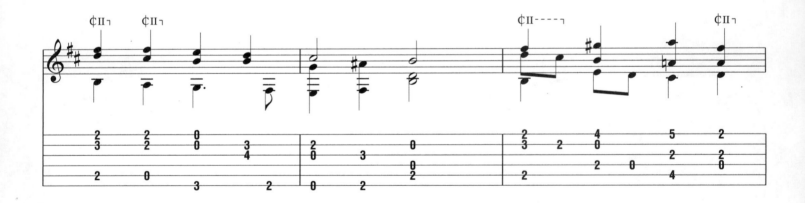

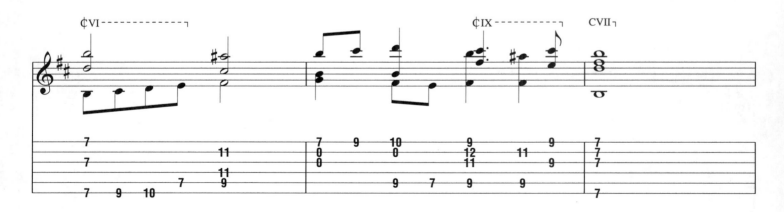

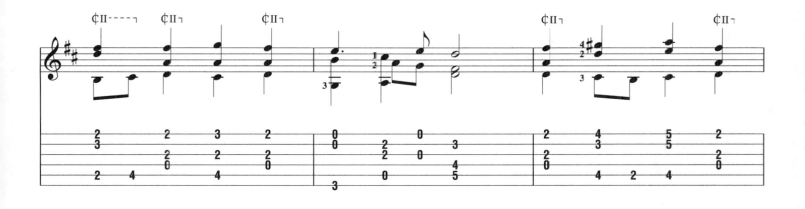

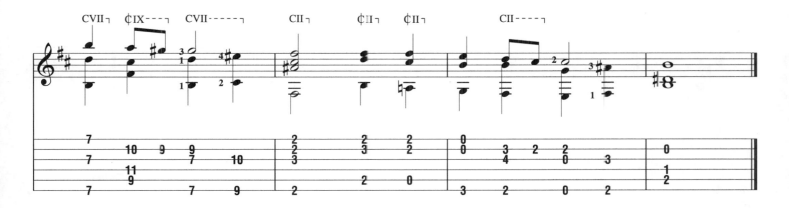

The Harmonious Blacksmith

George Frederick Handel

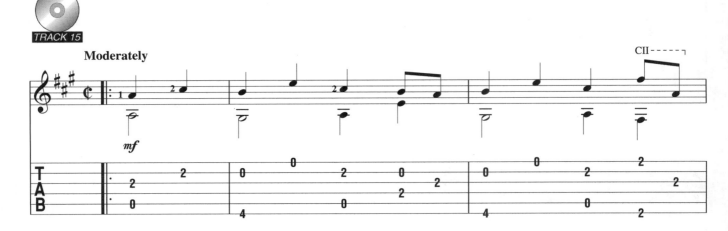

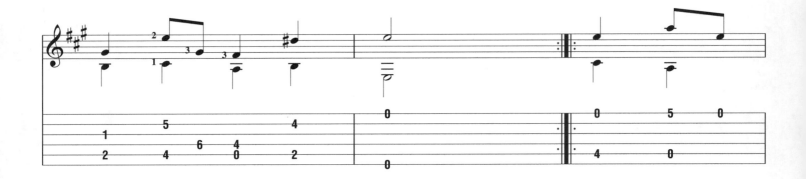

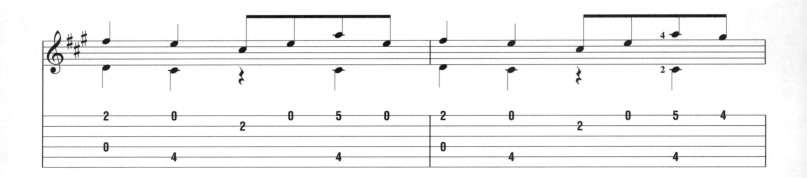

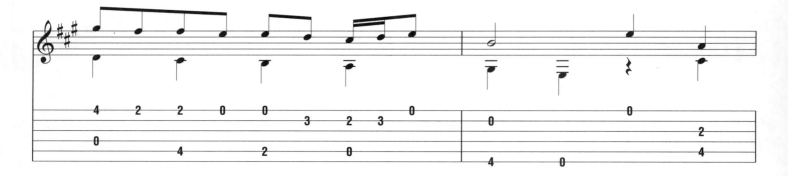

Gavotte

George Frederick Handel

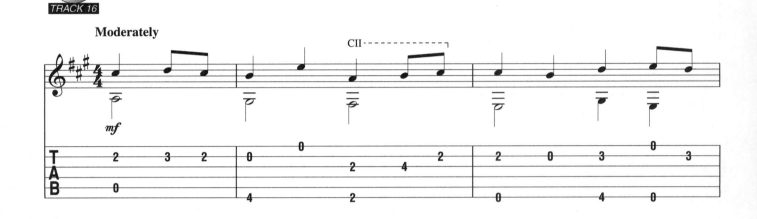

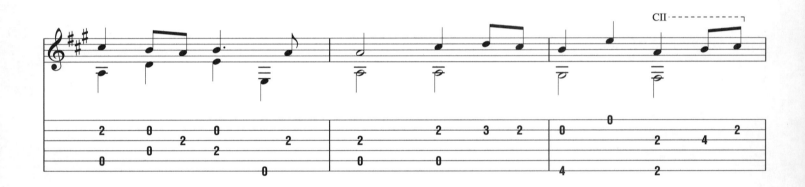

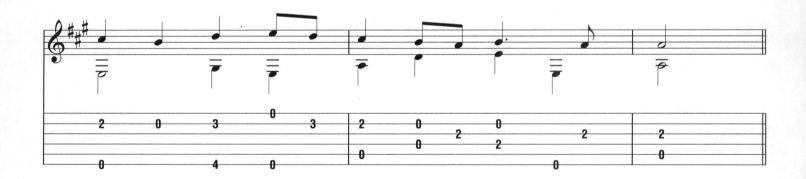

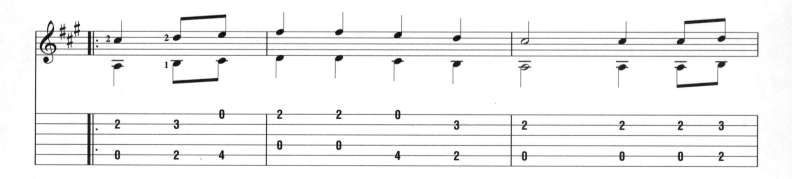

Sarabande

George Frederick Handel

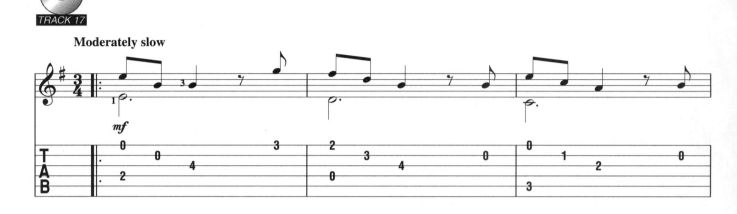

Moderately slow

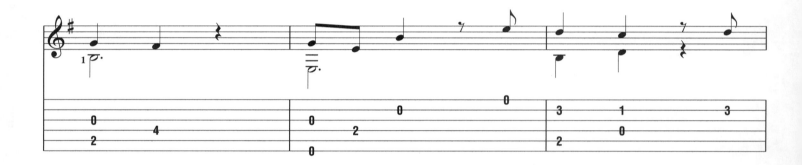

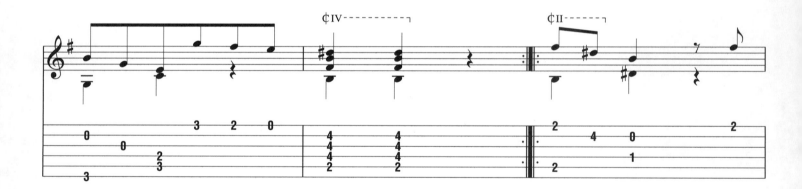

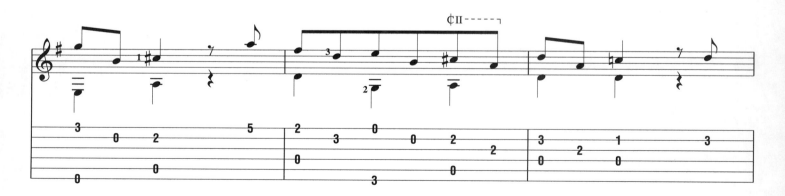

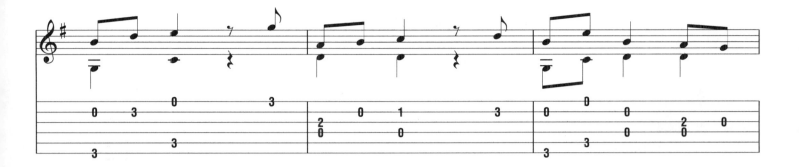

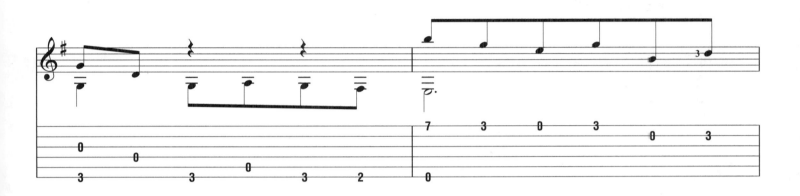

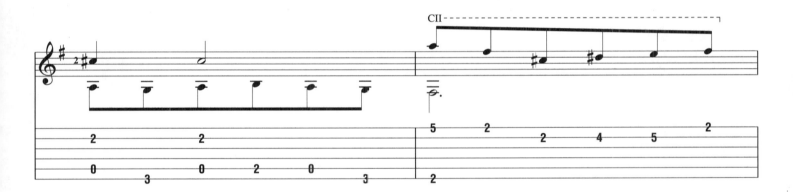

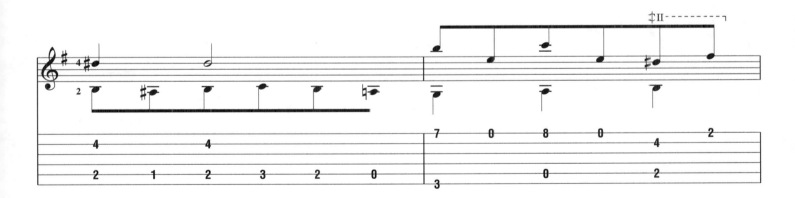

Minuet

George Frederick Handel

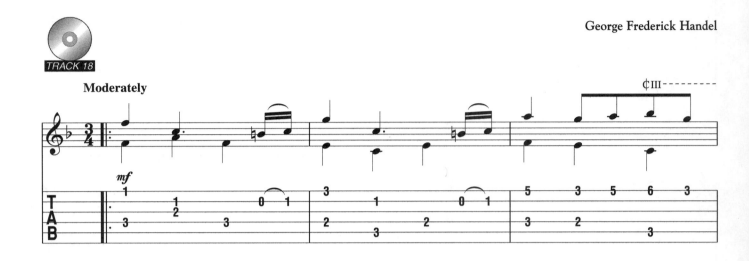

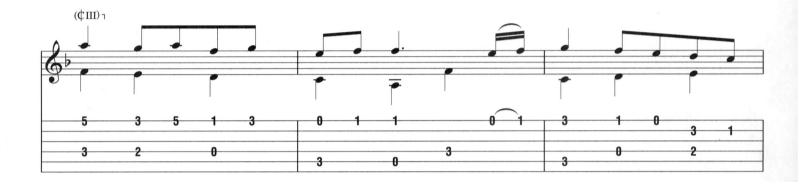

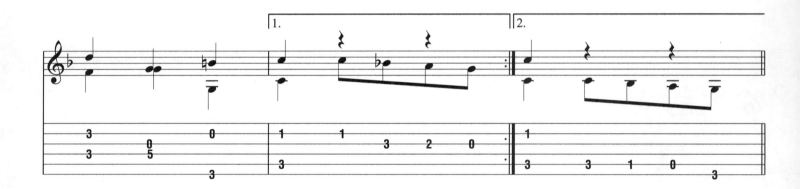

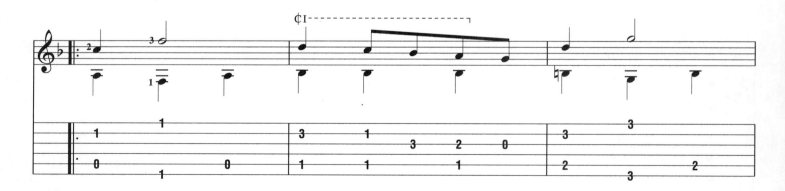

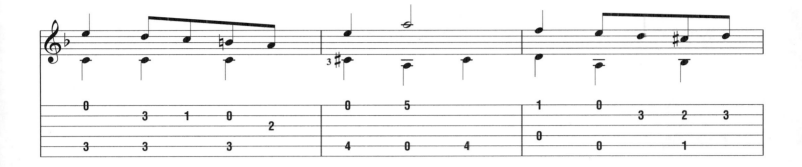

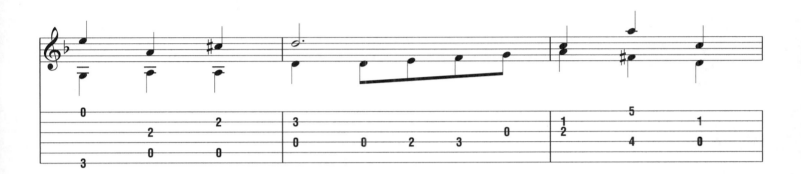

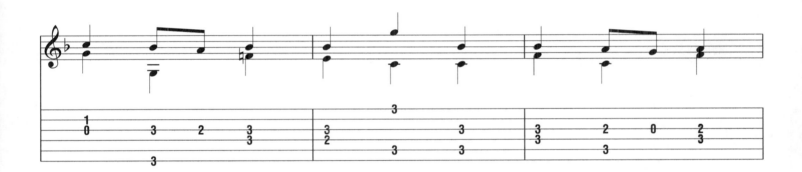

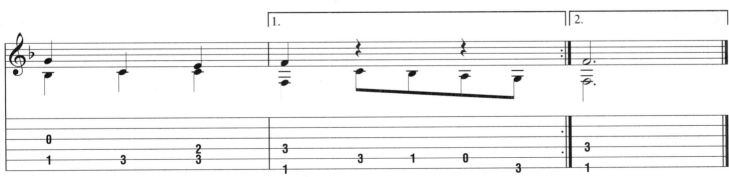

Adagio 1

George Frederick Handel

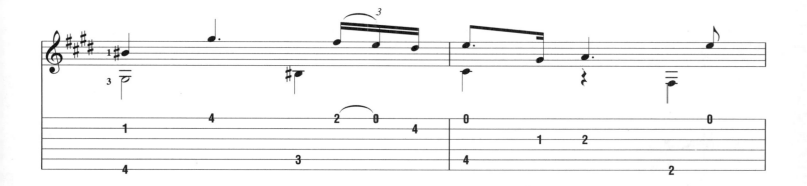

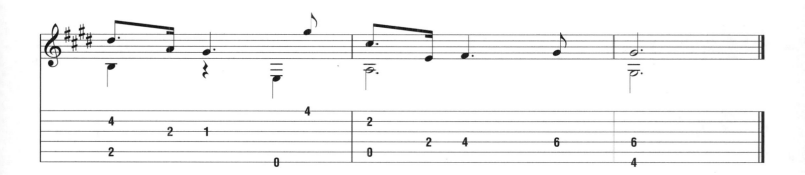

Adagio 2

George Frederick Handel

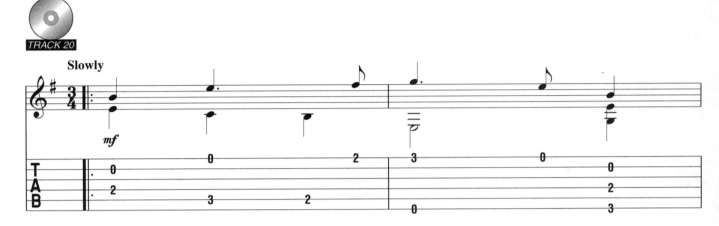

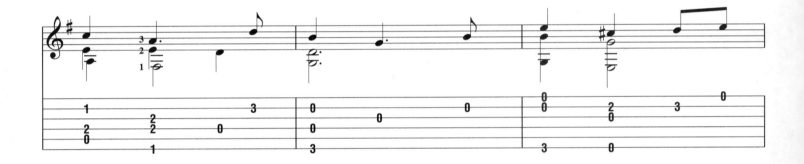

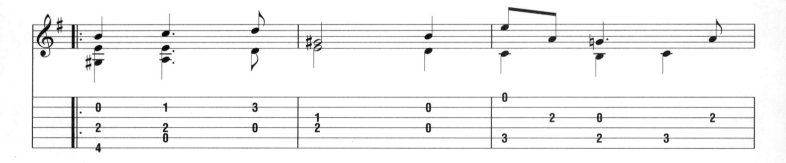

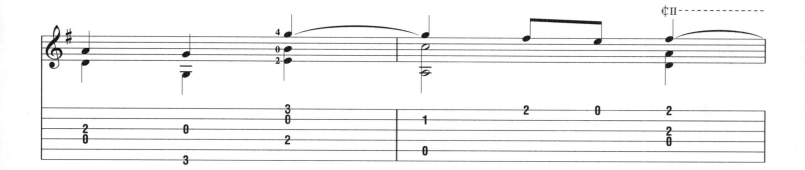

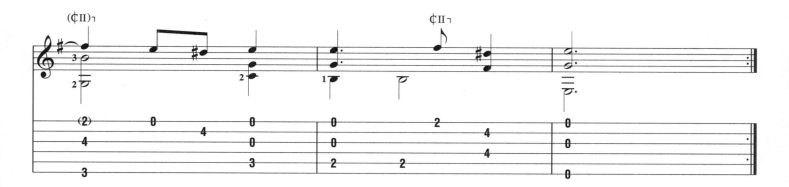

Adagio 3

George Frederick Handel

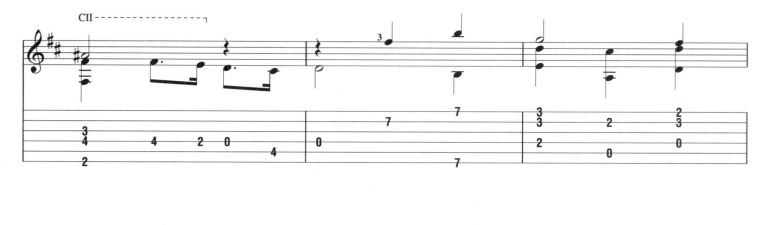

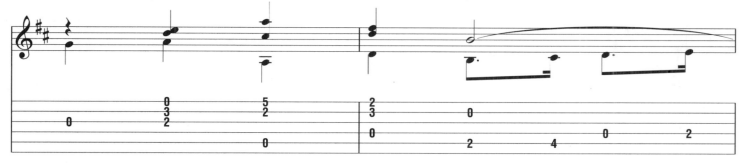

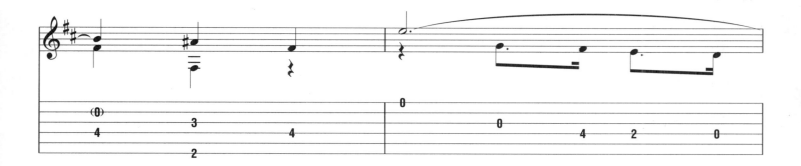

Bourrée 1

George Frederick Handel

TRACK 22

Moderately

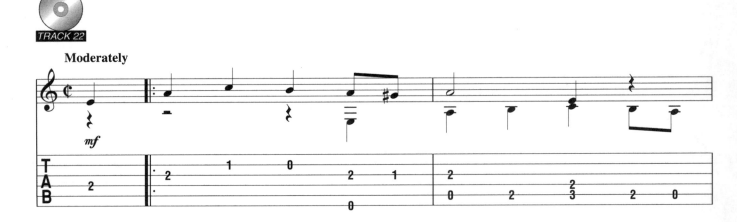

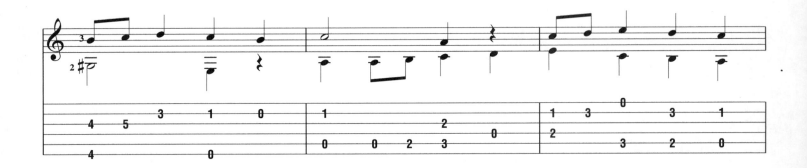

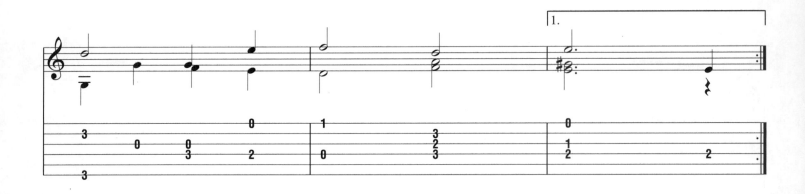

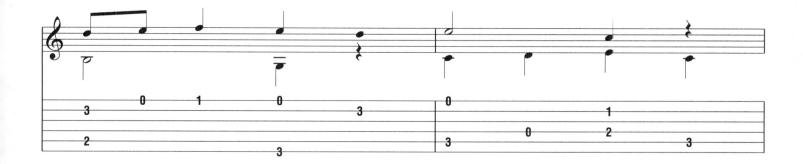

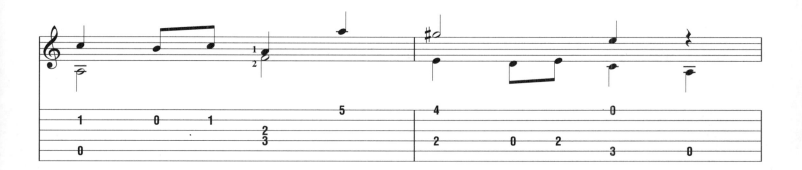

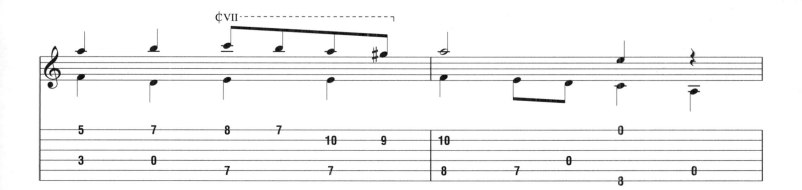

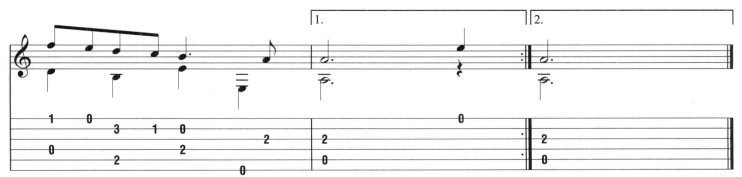

47

Bourrée 2

George Frederick Handel

TRACK 23

Tune 6th string to D

Moderately

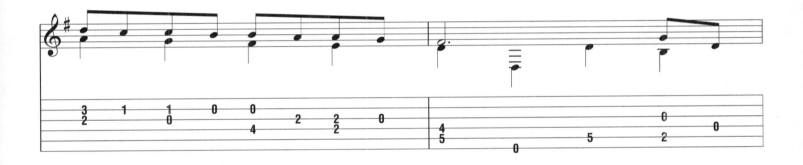

Bourrée 3

George Frederick Handel

TRACK 24

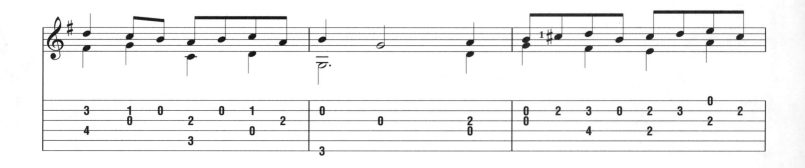

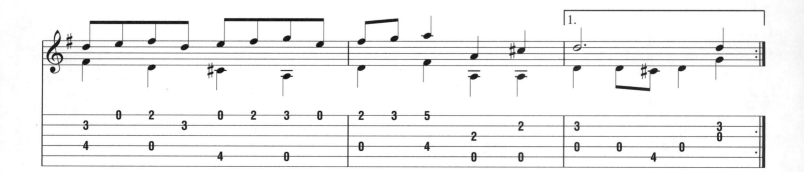

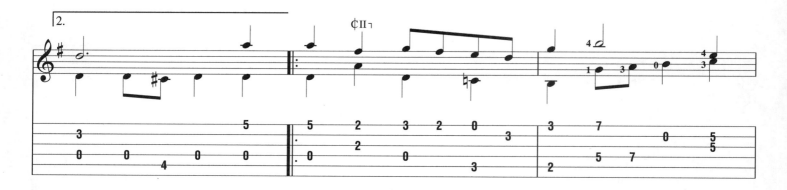

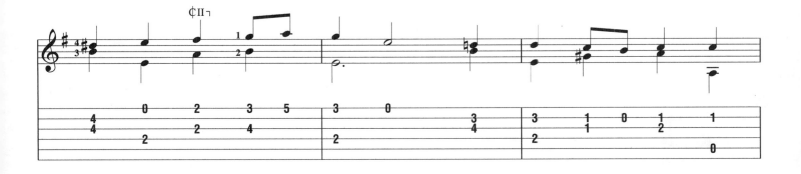

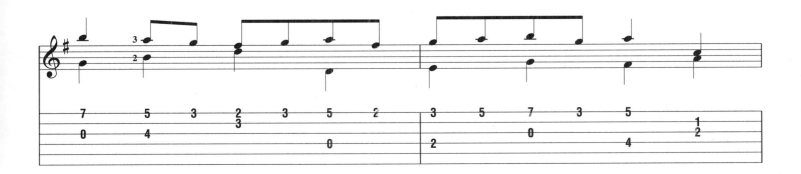

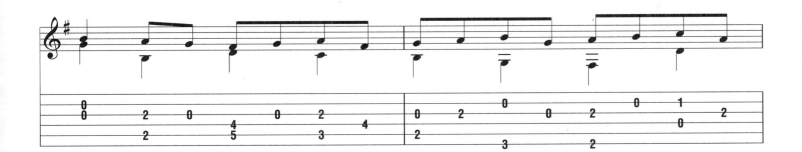

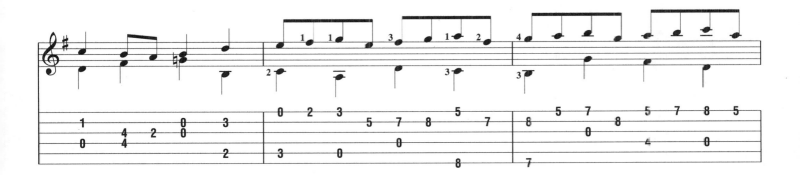

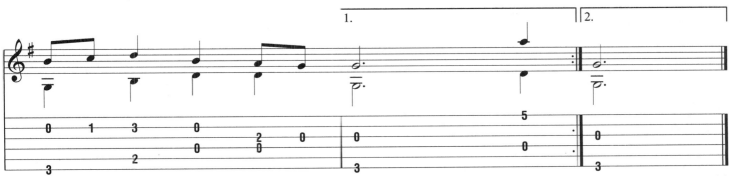

Allegro 1

George Frederick Handel

TRACK 25

Moderately fast

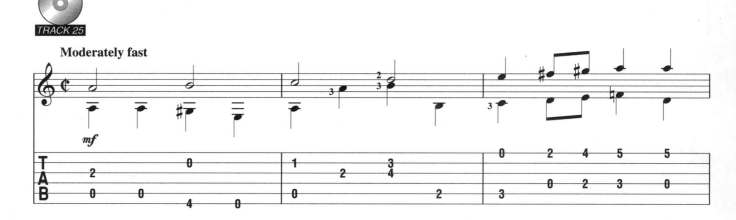

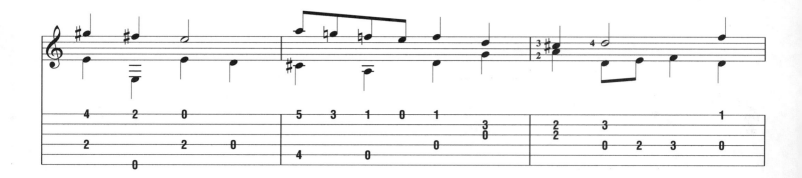

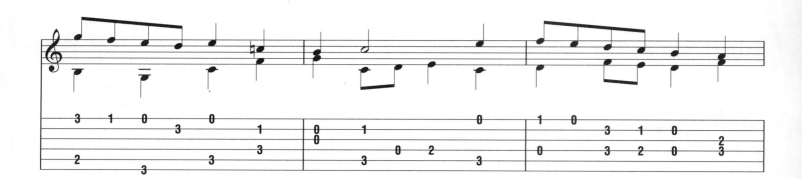

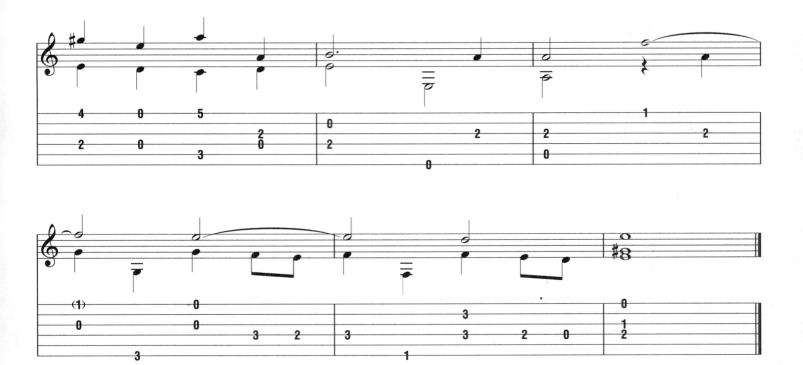

Allegro 2

George Frederick Handel

Moderately fast

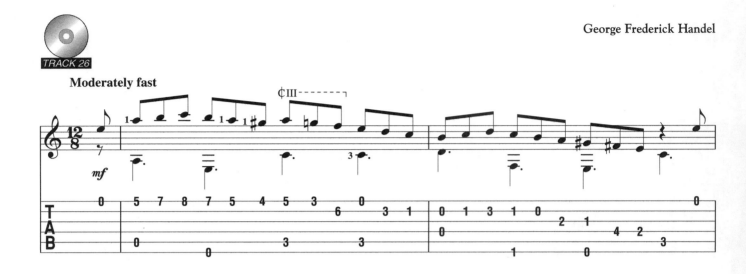

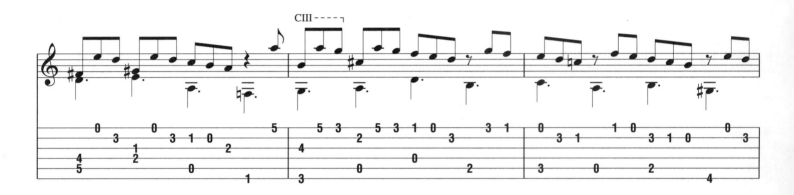

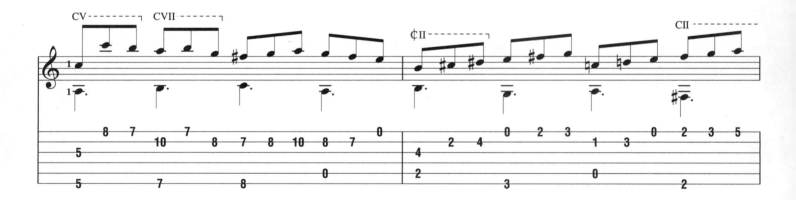

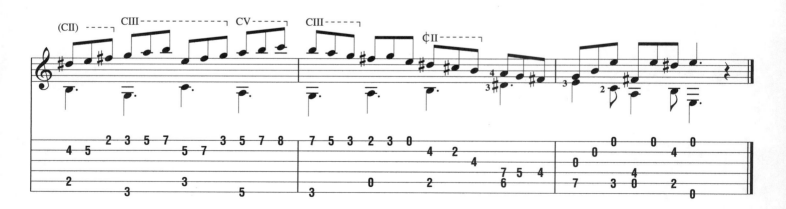

Andante

George Frederick Handel

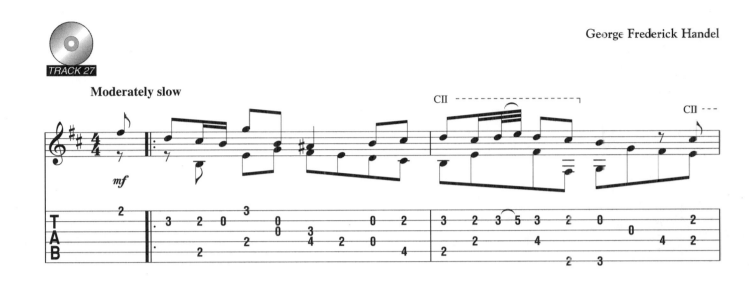

Moderately slow

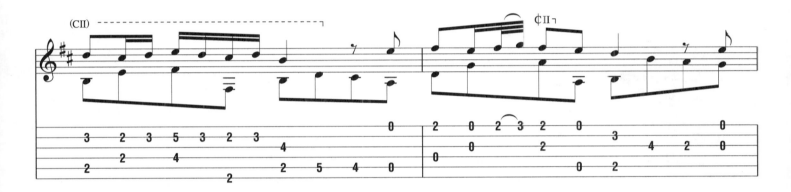

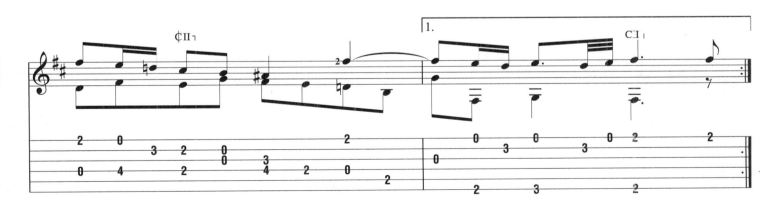

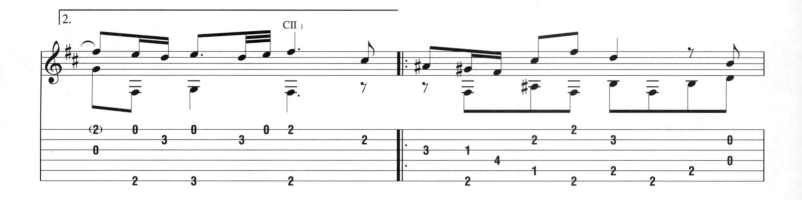

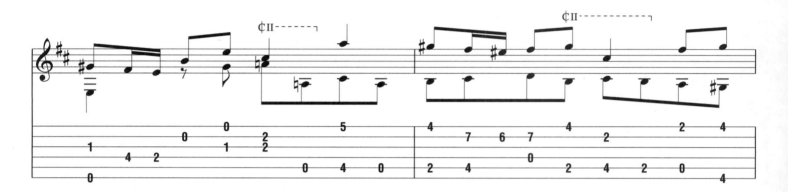

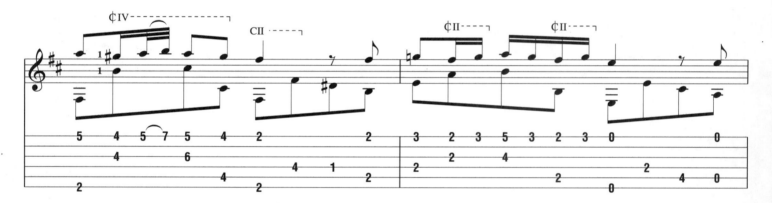

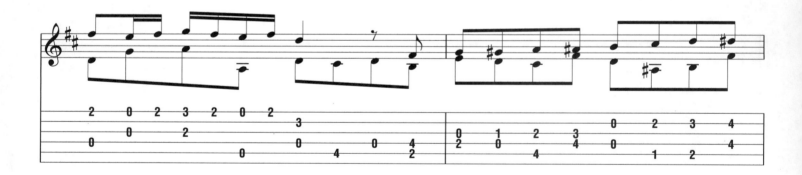

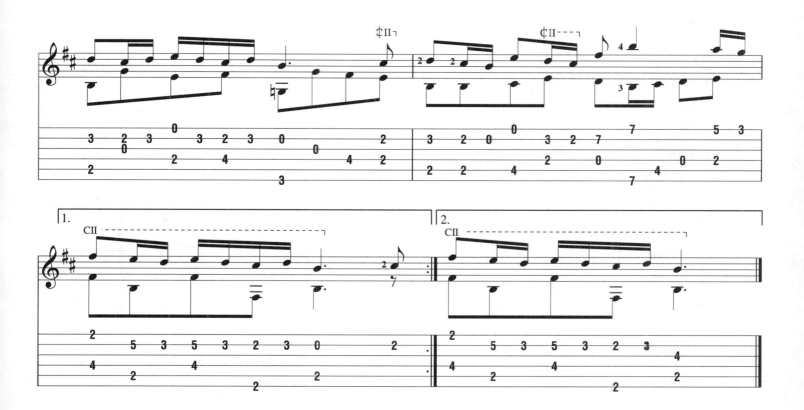

Theme

Wolfgang Amadeus Mozart

TRACK 28

Moderately fast

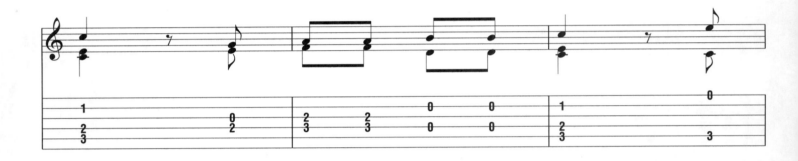

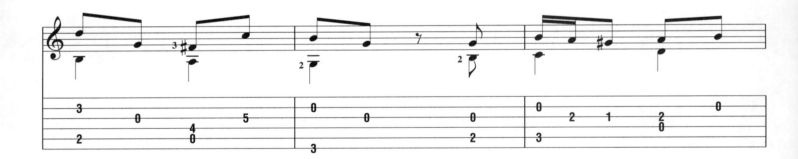

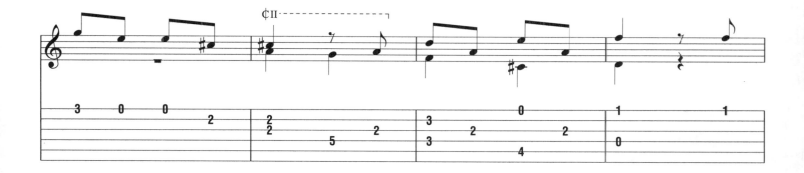

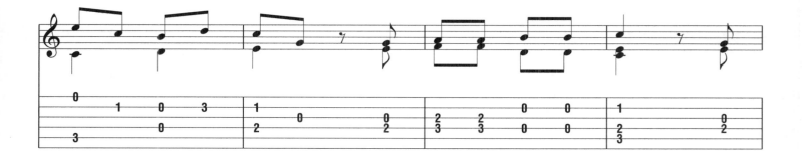

Minuet 1

Wolfgang Amadeus Mozart

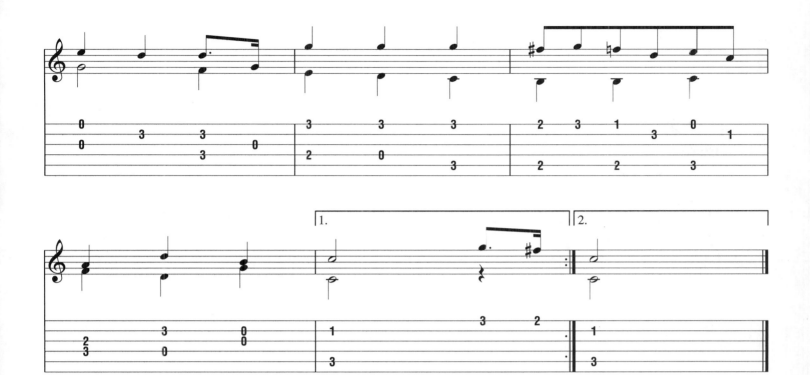

Minuet 2

Wolfgang Amadeus Mozart

Minuet 3

Wolfgang Amadeus Mozart

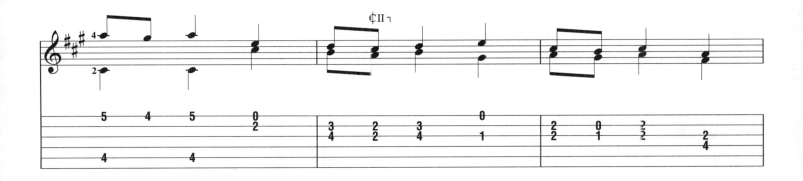

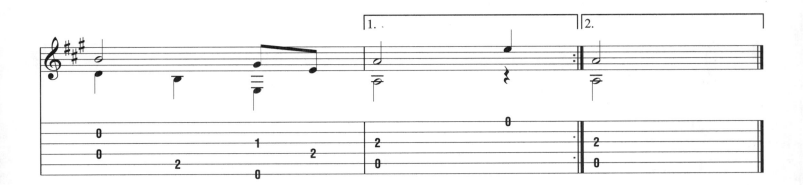

Minuet 4

Wolfgang Amadeus Mozart

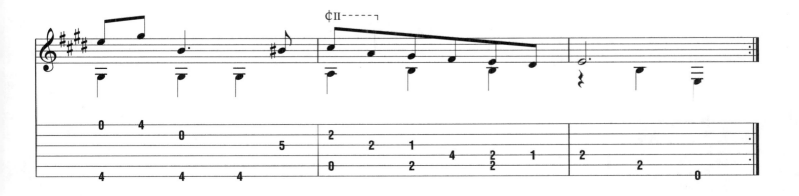

Minuet 5

TRACK 33

Wolfgang Amadeus Mozart

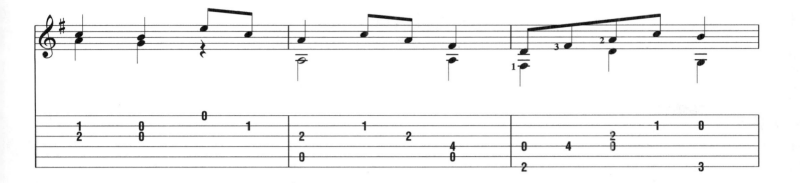

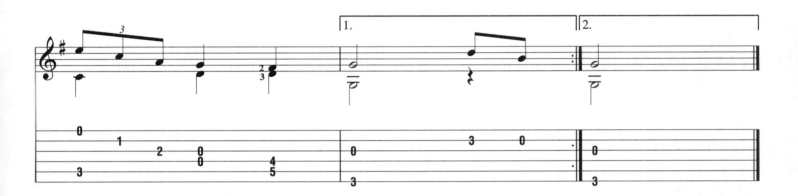

Minuet 6

Wolfgang Amadeus Mozart

Minuet 7

Wolfgang Amadeus Mozart

TRACK 35

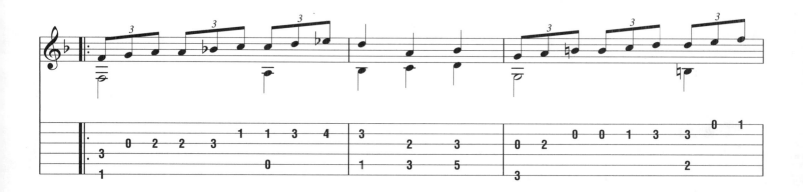

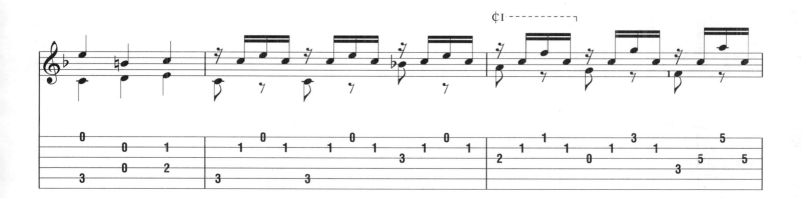

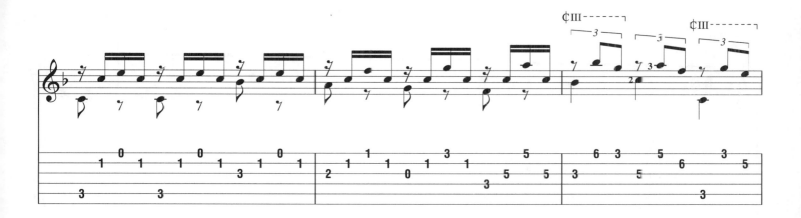

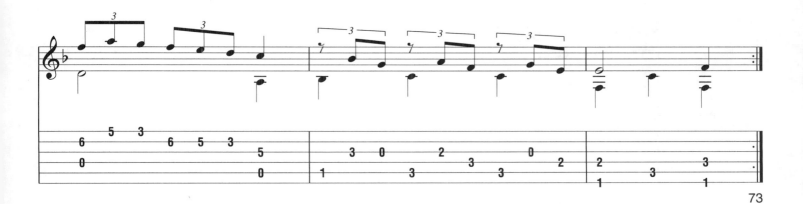

Trio 1

Wolfgang Amadeus Mozart

Trio 2

Wolfgang Amadeus Mozart

TRACK 37

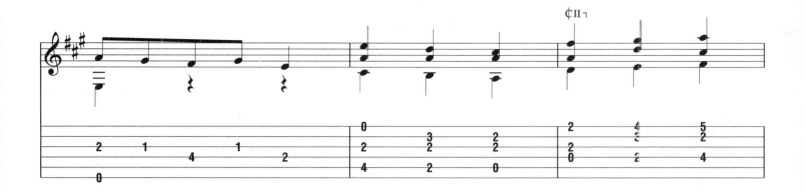

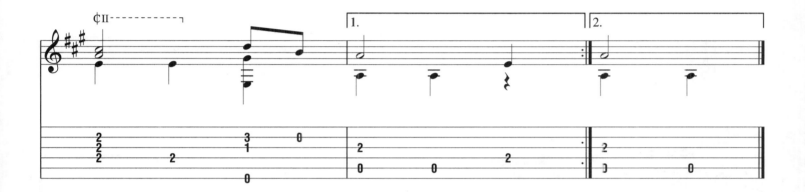

Andante 1

Wolfgang Amadeus Mozart

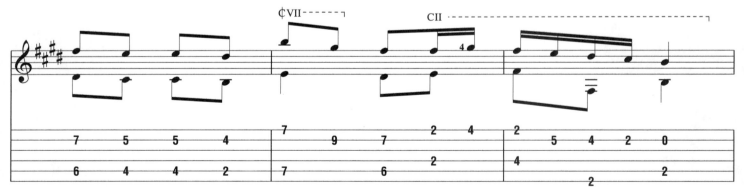

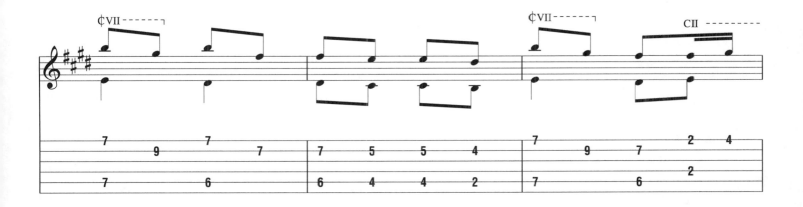

Andante 2
(2nd Movement Theme)
from Piano Concerto No. 20

Wolfgang Amadeus Mozart

TRACK 39

Moderately slow

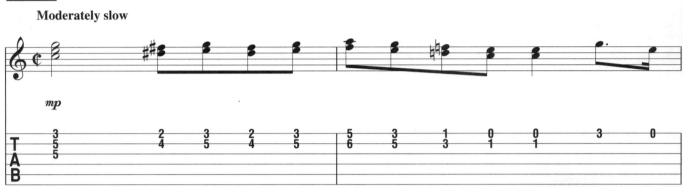

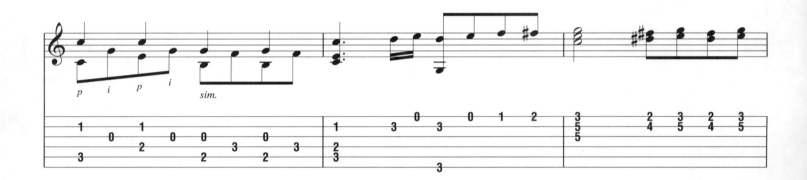

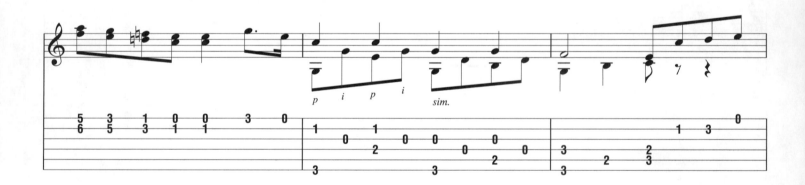

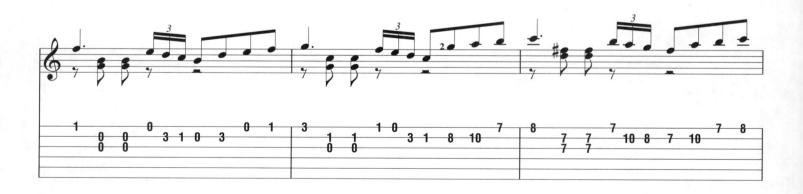

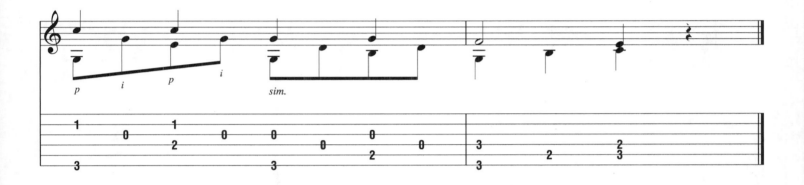

Andante 3
(2nd Movement Theme)
from Piano Concerto No. 15

Wolfgang Amadeus Mozart

TRACK 40

Moderately slow

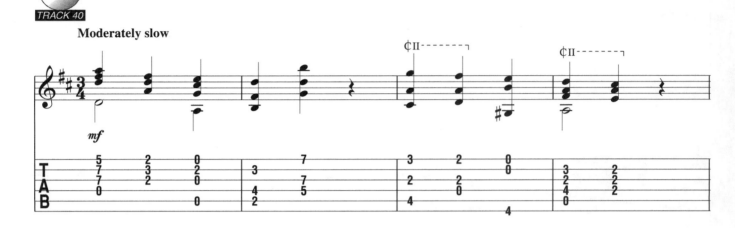

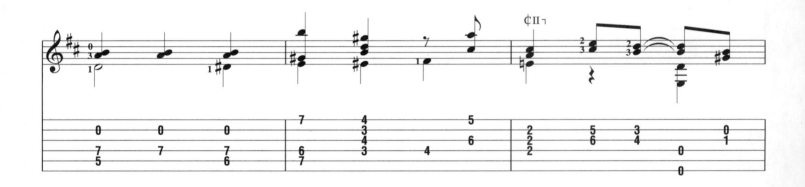

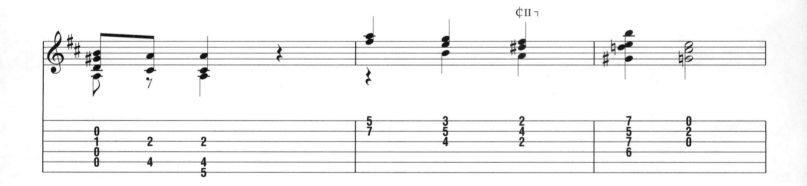

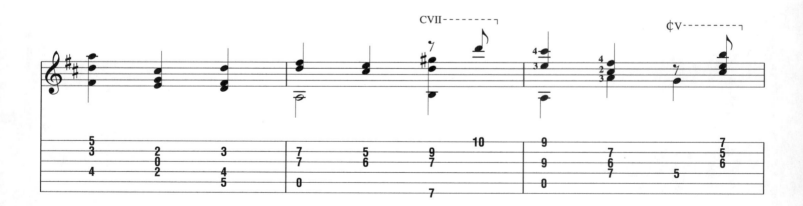

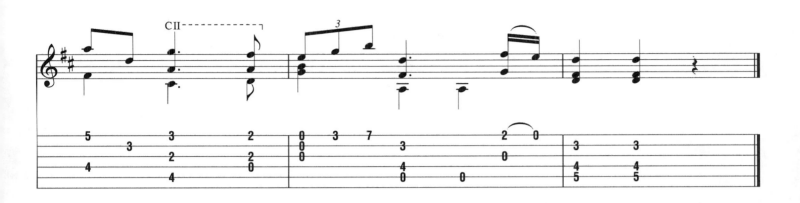

Allegro
(1st Movement Theme)
from Piano Concerto No. 13

Wolfgang Amadeus Mozart

Moderately fast

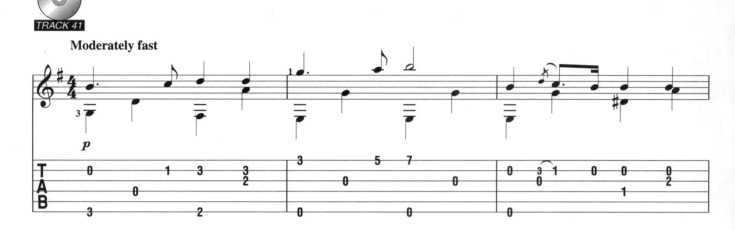

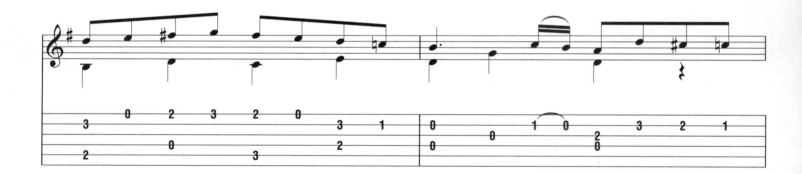

Russian Folk Tune

Ludwig van Beethoven

TRACK 42

Brightly

Pretty Minka

Ludwig van Beethoven

German Dance 1

Ludwig van Beethoven

German Dance 2

Ludwig van Beethoven

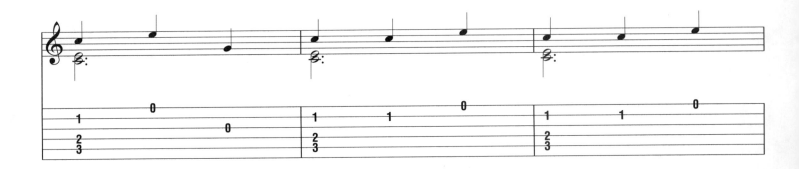

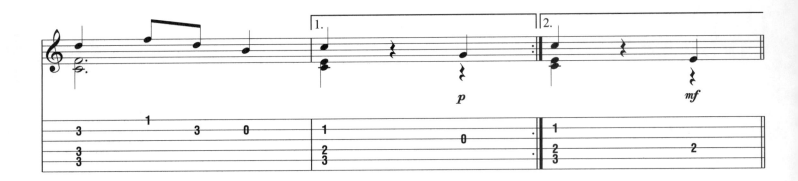

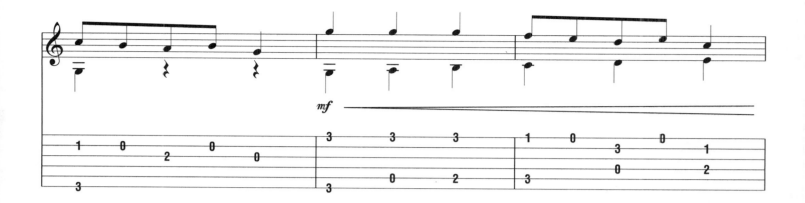

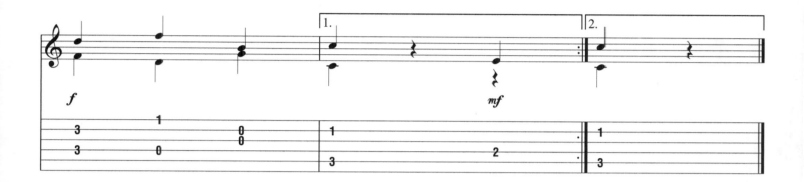

Ecossaise

Ludwig van Beethoven

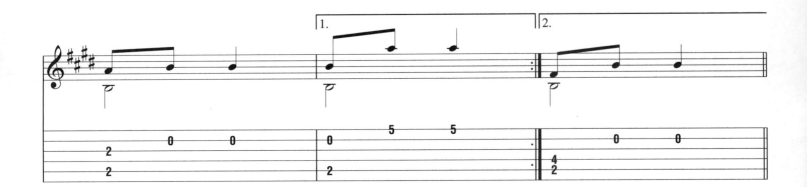

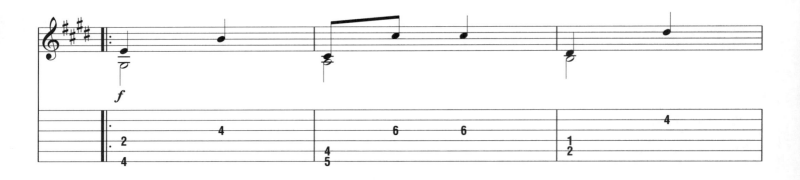

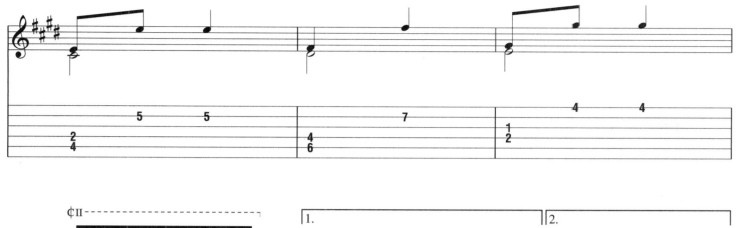

Country Dance

Ludwig van Beethoven

Moderately fast

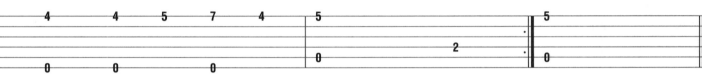

Ländler
(Tyrolean Air)

Ludwig van Beethoven

TRACK 48

Tune 6th string to D
and 5th string to G

Moderately

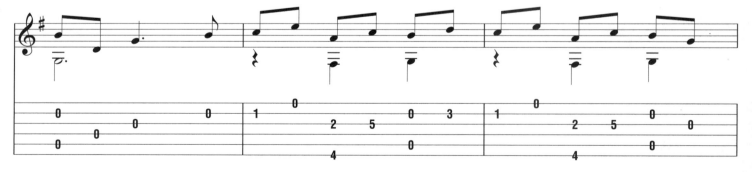

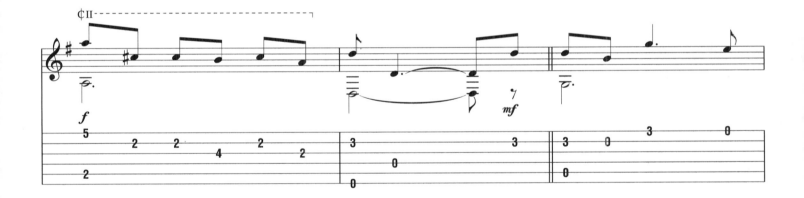

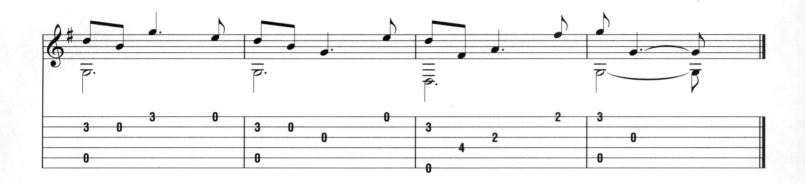

Ode to Joy

Ludwig van Beethoven

Dance

Ludwig van Beethoven

TRACK 50

Moderately, sadly

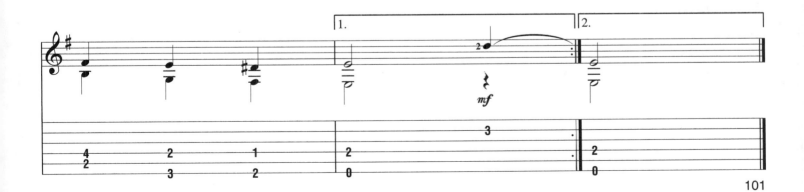

Minuet 1

Ludwig van Beethoven

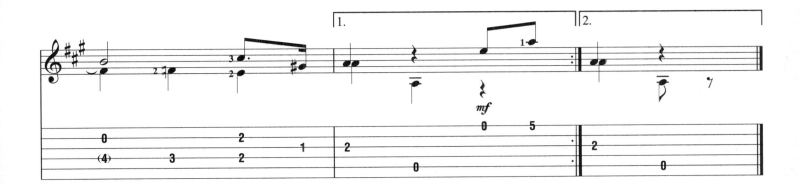

Minuet 2

Ludwig van Beethoven

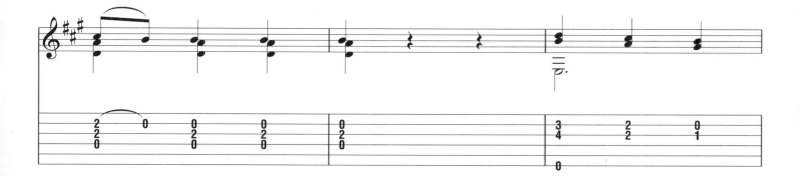

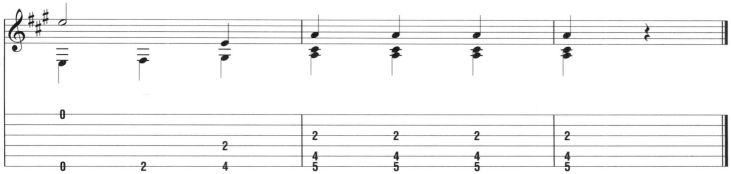

Bagatelle 1

Ludwig van Beethoven

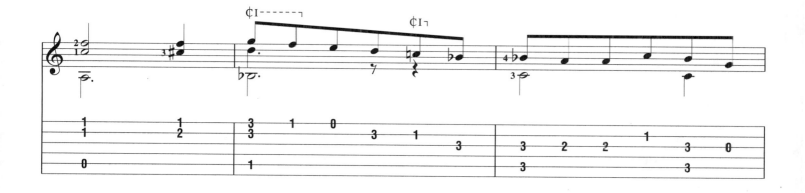

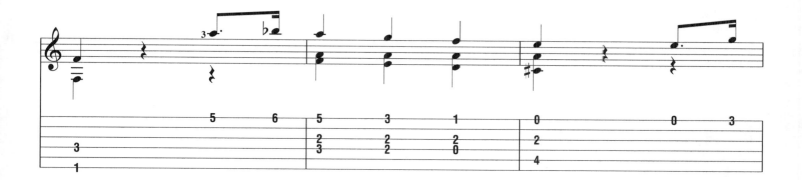

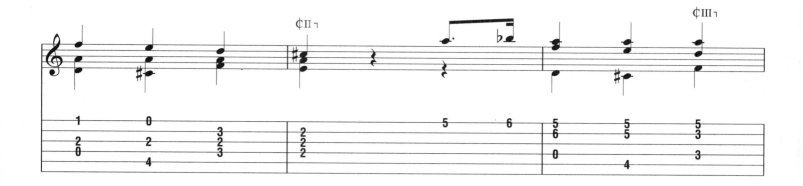

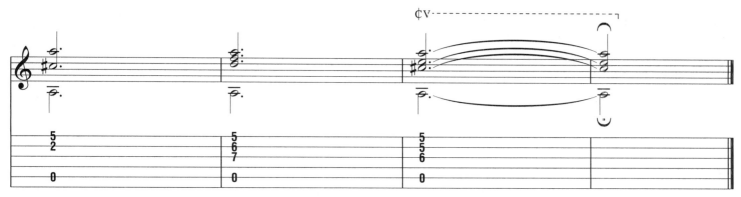

Bagatelle 2

Ludwig van Beethoven

TRACK 54

Slowly

Theme

Ludwig van Beethoven

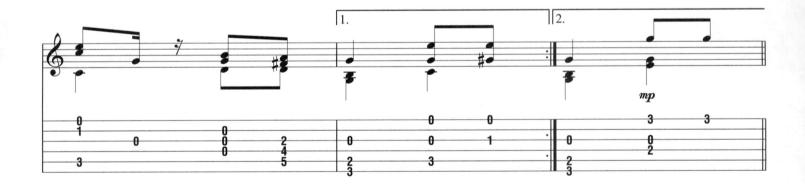

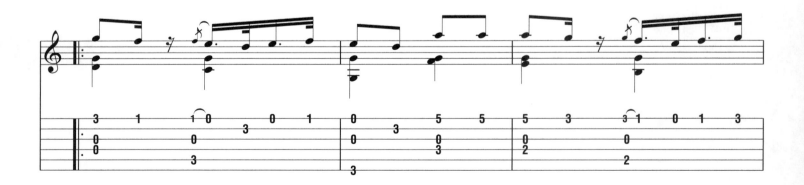

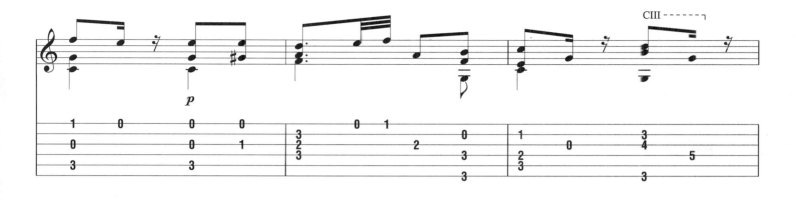

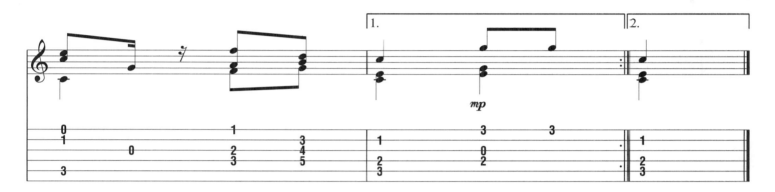

Lullaby

Johannes Brahms

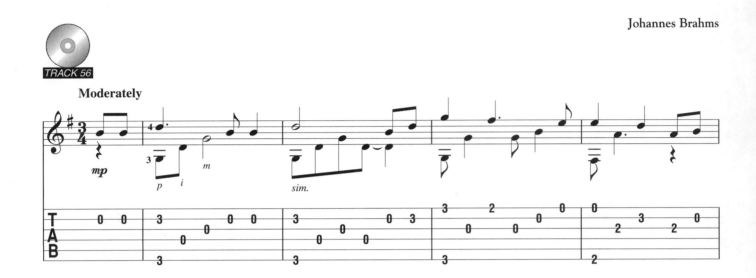

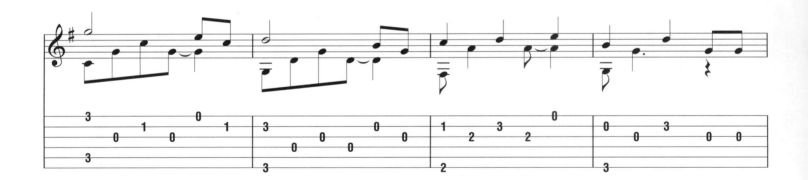

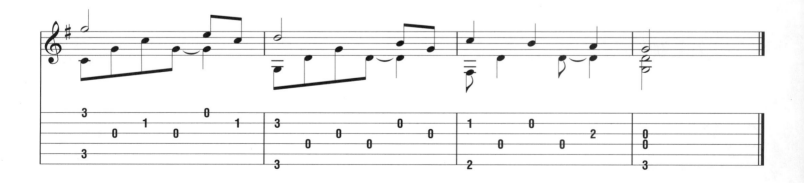

Symphony No. 3
(3rd Movement Theme)

Johannes Brahms

TRACK 57

Moderately slow

Waltz 1
(Op. 39, No. 2)

Johannes Brahms

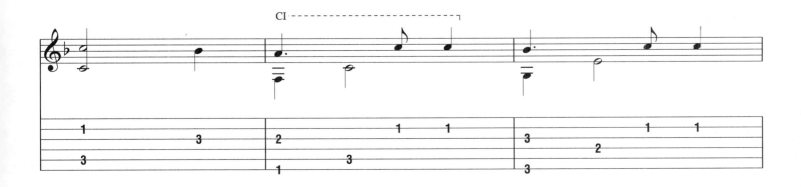

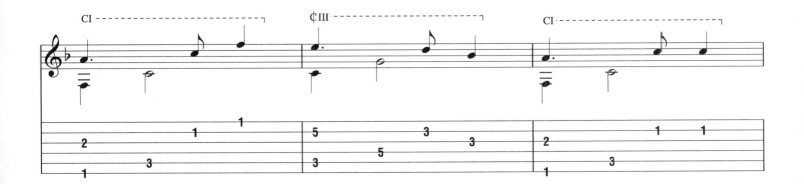

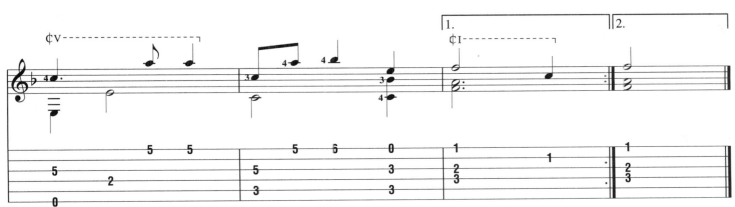

Waltz 2
(Op. 39, No. 15)

Johannes Brahms

Like a Melody

Johannes Brahms

Moderately, tenderly

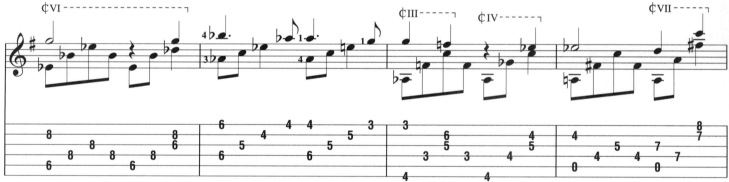

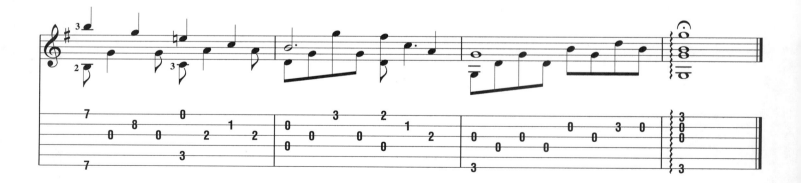